T0077914

THE ENTREPRENEUR'S SURVIVAL HANDBOOK

A Deck of 52 Insightful Pointers From an Experienced Entrepreneur

DERRECK FORD

BALBOA.PRESS
A DIVISION OF HAY HOUSE

Balboa Press books may be ordered through booksellers or by contacting:

Balboa Press
A Division of Hay House
1663 Liberty Drive
Bloomington, IN 47403
www.balboapress.com
844-682-1282

Because of the dynamic nature of the Internet, any web addresses or links contained in this book may have changed since publication and may no longer be valid. The views expressed in this work are solely those of the author and do not necessarily reflect the views of the publisher, and the publisher hereby disclaims any responsibility for them.

The author of this book does not dispense medical advice or prescribe the use of any technique as a form of treatment for physical, emotional, or medical problems without the advice of a physician, either directly or indirectly. The intent of the author is only to offer information of a general nature to help you in your quest for emotional and spiritual well-being. In the event you use any of the information in this book for yourself, which is your constitutional right, the author and the publisher assume no responsibility for your actions.

Any people depicted in stock imagery provided by Getty Images are models, and such images are being used for illustrative purposes only. Certain stock imagery © Getty Images.

Print information available on the last page.

ISBN: 978-1-9822-6003-3 (sc)
ISBN: 978-1-9822-6005-7 (hc)
ISBN: 978-1-9822-6004-0 (e)

Library of Congress Control Number: 2020924175

Balboa Press rev. date: 12/17/2020

This book is dedicated to
my daughter, Nadiyah

*You are the gift from the Creator who just
keeps giving, and I am so proud of you.*

"The greatest success we'll know, is helping others succeed and grow."

-- Greg Reid

CONTENTS

PREFACE

Entrepreneurship can be a risky endeavor and is not for everyone. For those choosing an entrepreneurial path, I believe it is important for them to have a guide, a survival handbook that will expose them to potential problems and ways to deal with them during their journey. There are a plethora of books and information available on how to start a business. What I found missing were the stories and challenges entrepreneurs face that are not common knowledge or openly discussed.

The information found in this Handbook is based on my experiences as an entrepreneur for 30+ years. Using this expertise, I co-founded JET Equipment Corporation, an African American-owned product identification equipment company, and I later founded JETEC Corporation.

I chose to provide fifty-two pointers so that the reader can pick a pointer each week, study it, and then record the desired actions or goals that were generated from studying the pointer. They can also treat them like a deck of cards, shuffle them up, and then select a pointer to study, discuss, and then set actions or goals.

This Handbook can also complement other textbooks used within college and university entrepreneurial programs. The information found within can be a valuable resource when starting a business, creating business plans, or performing consulting services for companies.

Let's get started by learning how I became an entrepreneur.

ACKNOWLEDGMENTS

I am grateful for the support that was given to me over my thirty-plus years as a business owner from a plethora of people. I am very appreciative of *Kindel Castle* for always believing in me and encouraging me to dream and to act. This handbook would not exist without her "you can do it" attitude toward this endeavor.

I thank the Creator for allowing me the opportunity to work with *James Johnson*, the most gifted software engineer whom I have ever known. Jim, you were before your time. Thank you for all your teachings and support.

Joseph O'Connor, I am indebted to you for your business guidance, financial assistance, and friendship. Thank you for exposing me to cornhole bean bag toss, although I still do not believe that it is truly a stress reliever.

I am blessed to have *Gary White* as a friend, professional role model, and mentor. Over the years, I often wish I heeded your wisdom earlier versus later.

James Zagorski, having a friend who is always available to assist in any way needed is invaluable. You are that friend and I appreciate you.

When my spirits were down, and I needed an external boost, I could always rely on *Howard Eaves*. As I have told you several times, you were -- and are -- my Bundini Brown.

When it comes to having the knack for bringing out the best in everyone they encounter, there is no one better to do this than *Scott Sorrell*. Scott, your passion for teaching is infectious, and I appreciate all the encouragement you gave in completing this handbook.

Bill Orak, we could not have reached as many worldwide companies without your help. When it comes to relationship selling, you are a master. Thank you for sharing your techniques.

Running a small business for any length of time requires the owner(s) to be true to their word. *Ray Guerrero*, you exemplified this mantra. I will always treasure our friendship.

Karl Reissmueller, you always told me that I was more than an engineer and you supported my dreams. I watched you lead at Hughes Aircraft Company, and it became clear that relationships with your personnel were the key to your success. You had a positive impact on so many from your organization. I am just one benefactor from your group.

There are other persons who, without their support, this handbook would not exist: *Hank Bode, Wally Hicks, Wayne and JR Williamson, Dr. Robert "Bob" Turner, Paul and Joyce Taylor* and *Cynthia Grant Peterson*. To the numerous employees of JET Equipment Corporation and JETEC Corporation, a sincere thank you for your contributions.

PROLOGUE
My Story:
How I Became an Entrepreneur

When did this desire first hit you? How deep did it resonate within your soul? For me, it happened when I was nine years old. I grew up in the Soundview Projects in the South Bronx, New York. Soundview is known as the birthplace of hip-hop music. *Afrika Bambaataa,* considered by many as the Father of Hip-Hop, commenced his hip-hop parties after my family left the projects for Newark, New Jersey. While living in the Bronx, I did all the things young New Yorkers did at the time: Played stickball, raised and raced pigeons, rode the subway, and shot water from the "Johnny Pump" (fire hydrant). My very first job was sweeping floors in a pharmacy. Later, at the excitement of seeing my older brother purchase a new bike with his paper route earnings, I decided to get one myself. I didn't mind delivering the morning newspapers, but I disliked having to do collections. Reflecting, I can see that I learned the art of rejection through collections. I would knock on the door and hear someone from behind the door say, "It's the paperboy!" Then someone else would say, "Tell him I'm not home!" The favorite line was, "Come back next week," or "I'm in a hurry right now but I will catch you next time." It was always pleasing when a customer would answer the door, pay their bill, and give me a tip. Those were my favorite customers, and I would make sure that I only approached them at reasonable times and gave them excellent service.

At our house, we grew up with the World Book Encyclopedia and Childcraft. Yes, we also had Funk & Wagnall's, but they weren't as pictorial as World Book. World Book had science projects that you could do on your own. I liked to visualize executing the projects. I finished some of them but most of the time I didn't have the monies to purchase the parts required so I would build them mentally. Perusing through the encyclopedias was a favorite pastime of mine. I learned about the different dog breeds, how many things worked, as well as the names of major companies producing automobiles, airplanes, toys, food, and commodities. I used to enjoy watching television commercials and hearing about new products or inventions, such as Good-n-Plenty, the food chopper, the microwave, McDonald's, and all the new Mattel toys, to name a few.

My mom would always come to me when something was broken in the house. I fixed clocks, radios, bicycles, you name it. What I couldn't figure out, I would research at the library or within the encyclopedias. I learned at an early age, that I had a knack for taking things apart and seeing how they fit back together. Realizing that I had this gift, I stated at the age of nine that I was going to start a company that helped companies improve their weaknesses. I called my imaginary company, "The Plant Doctors."

This drive to be a business owner – I didn't know it was called entrepreneurship at the time – directed the course of my academic career. I was always good at math. At one point, I pondered being a mathematician or an engineer but quickly chose engineering because engineers got to build things. People may not realize this, but engineers have contributed to almost every company in existence worldwide in some form or fashion. It is one of the fascinating professional disciplines that allows an engineer to work or live anywhere.

I attended Newark College of Engineering (NCE), which is now New Jersey Institute of Technology (NJIT). I graduated with a BS in Industrial Engineering and went to work for Armstrong World Industries in Lancaster, Pennsylvania. Armstrong was known for hiring industrial engineers to manage their various manufacturing plants. We did time and motion studies, cost control, recommended process improvements, established and maintained job descriptions, and so on. While in the employ of Armstrong, I realized that I enjoyed being a corporate engineer and that I also was rather good at it.

Many members of my family had moved across the country to Southern California. I visited Santa Monica after my junior year in high school. This was my first opportunity to travel by air and little did I know that I would be a regular airline traveler in the future. With my family in California I got the urge to "Go West," as well. I started to send out resumes to the various companies in Southern California: Mattel Toys, Northrop, Ford, Fluor Corporation, and Proctor & Gamble. I was offered a position at McDonald Douglas in Long Beach – also known as Douglas Aircraft Company (DAC). I took the position and moved to Westminster. Most of my duties involved performing time and motion studies that were never used. I learned quickly that my hiring was more centered on the company meeting Affirmative Action requirements and less on my potential contributions as an industrial engineer. Frustrated, I began seeking other employment and landed a position as a corporate engineer for Bergen Brunswig Corporation, a nationwide pharmaceutical distribution company. I traveled to their various distribution centers nationwide, assisting in improving the productivity of order picking and truck loading. After a while, the travel became too excessive for me, and I decided to find a local position that did not require travel.

During the 1980s, the electronics industry was beginning to boom in Southern California, especially in the Newport Beach and Irvine areas. I always shied away from electronic companies due to my struggles with Laplace transformations while attending engineering school. There was an excellent opportunity at Rockwell International in Newport Beach for an industrial engineer who would be part of an engineering team responsible for supporting their microelectronic fabrication lines, or "fabs." I took the position and became deeply knowledgeable about wafer fabrication: the process, the equipment required, the facility layout, and yields. Rockwell offered tuition reimbursement for their employees who pursued higher level degrees, so I started my MBA at Pepperdine University.

Things were going well for me at Rockwell until the entrepreneurial bug showed its head. The yields from the diffusion furnaces were not as desired. The cause was inconsistent ramping of the wafers into the furnaces due to faulty boat pullers. Wafers were placed on quartz boats and ramped into the oven using a sophisticated conveyor system referred to as boat pullers. After an engineering review of the problem, the corrective action was to either replace all the diffusion furnaces with newer models featuring advanced boat pullers or attempt to replace the boat pullers on all the existing furnaces. Unfortunately, the newer, advanced boat pullers could not be retrofitted to the older style furnaces and there were no boat puller replacements available for the current furnaces.

A fellow engineer and I decided that we would, on our own time and away from work, design and fabricate replacement boat pullers and sell them to Rockwell. Obviously, we did not think this through properly, but what the heck, we were engineers that were about to become entrepreneurs! We created a company called *Initiative Enterprises*, structured it as a partnership, filed a fictitious name, opened a bank account, borrowed $10,000 from my partner's dad and commenced engineering our boat puller. For this discussion, we will refer to it as "Model X." I recall my partner spending a lot of time creating a logo for Initiative Enterprises, with the final proof looking like a chess piece. As industrial engineers, we knew how to build a robust and replicable model. We sent a quote into purchasing, which was forwarded to the equipment maintenance team for review. They requested that we test and deliver a demo unit before they would commit to converting all their diffusion furnaces with the Model X. We fabricated the first unit and shipped it to Rockwell. It was installed and tested by the maintenance team, as well as the process engineering staff. The decision was made to procure additional units to replace the existing boat pullers.

From there, we received a purchase order for the additional units. Our excitement was short-lived because Purchasing learned that they were buying equipment from employees of Rockwell; this was against company policy. The P.O. was terminated, and my fellow engineer and I were fired.

I was then offered a position by the diffusion furnace manufacturer but opted not to accept. The CEO of the company was a former executive from Rockwell. He told me during my interview that he was impressed with my entrepreneurial spirit, although I had not gone about addressing that opportunity in the right manner.

Around this time, a former Director of Rockwell had moved over to Hughes Aircraft Company in Newport Beach. He was aware of my performance as an engineer, so I contacted him to see if there were any positions available for me at Hughes. He was responsible for the wafer fabrication business unit and offered me a position as a process engineer. There was also a position for a process engineer within the hybrid microelectronic business unit. The hybrid business was growing, and

Hughes was building a new facility, Building E, on their existing site. I was offered a position as a process engineer, supporting the hybrid business unit, as well. I had already been part of a team at Rockwell responsible for creating a brand-new wafer fab, Fab 4, so I was eager to learn something new. I chose to accept the position with the hybrid microelectronic facility. Luckily, Hughes also offered tuition reimbursement, so I was able to continue my MBA program.

I became a member of the Advanced Automation Group at Hughes. This group consisted of approximately ten to twelve individuals of different disciplines. We were handed the responsibility of identifying and implementing advanced hybrid manufacturing techniques within the new hybrid facility. I was responsible for what was referred to the "back end," which consisted of the processes from cover seal to burn-in, including environmental testing. One of the processes was cover marking or Ident.

One of the members of the group had attended a trade show and saw an inkjet system marking cans and thought a modified version of this system might be feasible for the marking of hybrid microelectronic chips. He pursued the manufacturer and purchased a modified version for Hughes Aircraft, Newport Beach. Upon its arrival he worked on it to have it qualified for production and then I was responsible for implementing. The system had many quirks and over time new inkjet printers became available from multiple vendors. By now, I was heading the Advanced Automation Group. I supervised both software and mechanical engineers and was responsible for assigning their projects. One of the projects assigned was a redesign of the first inkjet system. We were able to take an inkjet from one manufacturer and the ink and fluid from another competitor manufacturer, and then integrate them together with an XY plotter to create an advanced inkjet marking system. This system worked so well that three of them were configured, one for each of the hybrid production areas.

At that time, Hughes had an equipment group in Carlsbad. Their primary product lines were wire bonders and die attach machines, but I thought that there may be an opportunity for them to add the inkjet systems to their product lines. The idea was reviewed by the Carlsbad management team and declined. At this point, I had another entrepreneurial moment.

Video rental stores were becoming exceedingly popular at the time (this was before Blockbuster) and one of my software engineers and I thought of creating software to help manage video store inventories and membership. I mentioned to him my thoughts of creating a new inkjet marking system that could be sold to hybrid manufacturers nationwide. The software, hardware, and system configuration would be different than the one presently used at Hughes. I knew that I needed my software engineer and a technician, who knew how to service the inkjet printers. I approached the software engineer first, telling him that I wanted to start a business selling integrated industrial inkjet printers; he was on board. We both knew who we wanted as the third person, a knowledgeable technician. We approached him, and he wanted to be a part of the team, too.

We started meeting after work at the home of one of the team members. We discussed system configuration, software requirements, company structure, company name, ownership percentages (I was adamant that I had no less than 51 percent ownership to ensure we maintained a minority-owned business status), duties, and pricing. A few years prior, I created a sole proprietorship, Ford & Associates, which allowed me to accept any type of consulting or private contract work. Using the Ford & Associates name, I performed a test market by sending out questionnaires to process engineers at various hybrid facilities around the country. I received a 21 percent response and 100 percent interest in a computer-controlled inkjet parts marking system. It was now time for me to create a business plan. The three-year pro forma revealed the cash requirements to start the business. Part of the first-year cash requirements included the cost to procure the materials necessary to build our demo inkjet system.

The next step was for me to talk with senior management at Hughes about my idea to start my own company and to file a conflict of interest proposal. I knew that if I started a company to sell industrial ink jet systems that I would have to leave my position at Hughes. The Director of Hybrid Manufacturing at the facility had been very fair to me over the years and I viewed him as a mentor, therefore, I spoke to him about my intentions. He told me that Simon Ramo, one of the founders of TRW, was a former Hughes Aircraft Company employee and that Hughes looked highly on individuals who wanted to exercise their entrepreneurial flair. I gave him a copy of my conflict of interest proposal and was told that he would give it to Hughes counsel. I waited a short time before learning that my conflict of interest proposal was signed and approved by

Hughes Corporate. I was free to proceed. JET Equipment Corporation was founded in March 1990.

Selecting a reliable motion assembly vendor to provide motion hardware was important to the initial success of our business. Unbeknownst to me and another partner, our third partner befriended a local motion assembly vendor who was looking to exit from his business and purchased that entity. In one of our meetings, he reported that he now owned a motion assembly company and that it could supply hardware for our new venture. I immediately informed him that he would have to sell his shares of JET and divorce himself from our new venture. An agreement was entered into and he was now free to focus on his newly acquired company. We parted on amiable terms, so he was still available and willing to provide us with technical assistance as required. In fact, we ended up purchasing the motion hardware for our first customer from his company. The quality and performance of his delivered system exceeded our expectations.

My partner and I continued to meet to create our first working prototype and to plan the launching of the business. With the business plan completed, our immediate goal was to obtain the $200,000 start-up capital that was identified in our business plan.

The most obvious source was a major inkjet manufacturer. It was clear to me that the inkjet supplier stood to benefit from the new enterprise that we were creating. Each time we sold a system, they sold a printer and fluids. Long term, they also received revenue for printer maintenance, replacement parts, and printer training. So, I contacted the president of one of the major ink jet manufactures and told him of my intent. He was extremely interested and wanted me to come to Illinois to discuss it further.

My partner and I went to Illinois and met with the president, his advisor, and the CFO of the inkjet manufacturer. We gave our pitch on how we would help them gain market share in the electronics industry, an industry where they did not have a significant presence, shared the results of our test market, and produced the signed conflict of interest proposal obtained from Hughes. We immediately received a favorable response. The quickness of this response startled me. I became cautious and back peddled. Knowing the use of funds that was identified in the business plan, I got the idea to ask for what was needed without having to give up corporate ownership. In the long-term, this proved to be a major and costly mistake. Once again, the president agreed to provide funds, not the total $200K, and set up extremely favorable payment terms on all printers and supplies purchased from his company by JET. We went home with a feeling of victory.

Over the next few months, we purchased all the components required to assemble our first prototype/sample system, finalized the software specs, and signed a lease for industrial space. I remained working at Hughes until we received our first purchase order. Using the savings that I had amassed from my 401(k), I left my position at Hughes and became the second employee of JET. My partner, a software guru, was the first employee.

We were able to become the standard within the electronics industry for inkjet parts marking systems worldwide, as well as implemented systems in non-electronic companies. Over the years, some of our customers included: Hughes Aircraft Company, Northrop Grumman, Raytheon, Motorola, Burr Brown, Teledyne, Texas Instruments, Anaren Microwave, Phillips, Aeroflex, Remec Defense, National Security Agency (NSA), Honeywell, 3COM, Compaq, Digital Equipment Corporation, Seagate Technologies, Boeing (including Boeing Electronics), Haagen-Dazs, Breyers & Edy's Ice Cream, Campbell Soup, Ford Motor Company, Nestle, Mattel Toys, Biosite, ASP, and Johnson & Johnson.

I am an African American Entrepreneur with over thirty years' experience owning a high-tech company in Orange County, California that manufactures digital product marking systems sold to industrial manufacturers worldwide. The lessons that I have learned as the "surviving" head of a minority-owned company over this period are priceless. I am sharing my experiences with the following intent:

- ◆ To inspire individuals to take that next step toward becoming an entrepreneur.
- ◆ To share information that is generally not taught in business schools.
- ◆ To provide entrepreneurs with long-term survival tools.
- ◆ To help entrepreneurs reach their goals while maintaining a balanced life.
- ◆ To provide weekly tips to help strengthen your mental resolve in becoming a successful entrepreneur and to identify areas within

your organization that may benefit from some of the lessons learned from my experiences. The deck is purposely presented in a random fashion. Each week randomly pick a pointer from the deck to read and to reflect upon. Try to write at least three actions or goals that you would like to achieve for each pointer selected and then take some action towards these goals before proceeding to another pointer.

+ To provide pointers within this handbook that enable entrepreneurs to start and run their businesses without making the same mistakes that I did and know that they have a high probability of being successful in their endeavors. If reading the pointers presented result in inner reflection or dialog among you and your team, then my objective has been reached. I believe that I have made enough mistakes as a business owner to cover the up and coming entrepreneurs.

I am a motivational speaker and entrepreneur coach, deeply passionate about entrepreneurism and engaging with my audience. I would be honored to speak at your high school, college, or company on topics relating to entrepreneurism. Visit my website at **www.dycmn.com** to schedule a speaking session or to request entrepreneurial coaching.

Derreck A. Ford
Motivational Speaker & Entrepreneur Coach
Founder DYCMN™ and Founder JETEC Corporation
derreck.ford@dycmn.com, PH: [949] 394-2107

You need a team because the burden of a big dream
is sometimes too much to shoulder on your own.
– Michael Hyatt

Establish an Advisory Board:
Create a Lifeline for Your Enterprise

The saying "No man or woman is an Island" should be embedded in the minds of all entrepreneurs. Yes, we run the show but that doesn't mean we have all the answers. I recommend establishing and updating your advisory board at every major stage of your company's growth. Your advisory board is not your "yes" group, but a collection of seasoned professionals who help you to make more informed decisions. In many cases, they are the professional talents who you currently do not have your payroll. Recommended advisory board skill sets include legal (corporate and contracts law), finance (including business financing and business taxation), business strategy, human resource, sales and marketing, and business start-up. Having an entrepreneur with a similar experience level as yourself on your board can also be invaluable. What's a comfortable advisory board size? I would say five to eight professionals.

The power of being able to confer with your advisory board and knowing you are accountable to them can be priceless. If I had put together an advisory board at the infancy stage of JET, I would have had professionals guide me through many initial aspects of the business. I am confident that the advisory board would have seen the benefits of the Fortune 1000 ink-jet manufacturer having partial ownership in my startup venture, and that in the long-run they would have had a vested interest in seeing the company grow. They would have advised me to give up a portion of the company's stock to create a stronger partnership.

Desired Actions or Goals I Will Take from Pointer 1

1. _____

_____

2. _____

_____

3. _____

_____

Everybody has a calling. And your real job in life is to figure out as soon as possible what that is, who you were meant to be, and to begin to honor that in the best way possible for yourself.
— Oprah Winfrey

Find Your Passion:
Do What Gives Meaning to Your Life

Passion is defined as an intense emotion, an overwhelming enthusiasm or desire for something. For me, it was to start an African American- or Black-owned high technology company that serviced manufacturers worldwide and provided a vehicle for young, motivated individuals to make a difference within a team environment. As a young adult, I would peruse *Black Enterprise* magazine's annual top 100 Black Owned Business listing. I knew each year what the annual sales revenue requirements were to make the listing. I established a sales revenue goal, and although I have not reached my goal after 30 years, I continue to strive to achieve it.

So, the key question you must ask yourself is, "Do you know what gives meaning to your life?" Is it being an active participant in your community, being of service to people, being the best partner you can be if in a relationship, having and demonstrating integrity, bringing something new to the world, having and spending time with your family, or creating wealth? It is important that you ask yourself this question because being an entrepreneur can be a time-consuming endeavor. There is an adage that goes, "When you love what you do there are not enough hours in a day to do what you want." If you let your enterprise consume your focus, time, and energy you will not be able to give those other meaningful areas of your life the attention they require. This can result in divorce, poor health, alcoholism, loss of friends, financial peril, and other catastrophes.

Finding balance between the business, home, health, and social activities is particularly important. I had to learn to be truly present with others when I am not at the office. There is a strong tendency to subconsciously work on business issues when away from the business. It helps that I have a passion for archery, basketball, and cycling, in addition to helping youth and being an active participant within my family and community. Having these strong interests allows me to counteract the impulse to work 24/7 on my business.

Desired Actions or Goals I Will Take from Pointer 2

1. _____

   _____

2. _____

   _____

3. _____

   _____

Accomplishing goals is not success. How
much you expand in the process is.
– Brianna West

Set Goals: *Write Them Down*

S uccessful entrepreneurs visualize and set goals. These goals are written down and shared with their team. Goal setting is an especially important trait to master. Your goals are your road map. Without them you have no substance for action or a measurement for success. Having goals will help you to stay focused, to keep your eyes on the prize (especially through adversity) and allow you to monitor progress of your actions.

I cannot stress enough the importance of writing down your goals. There is a power associated with written goals. It's as if once written down, there is a mental call to action. Once your goals have been written down, you can use such techniques as S.M.A.R.T. to create action plans to achieve said goals. Remember, to make your goals S.M.A.R.T., they need to conform to the following criteria: Specific, Measurable, Attainable, Relevant, and Timely.

Over the years, I maintained journals where I would write down my annual revenue, head count, industry segment, as well as sales and manufacturing related goals. I would then translate these goals to a format that I could share with my team. I would encourage my team to establish sub-goals where they would drill down from the top-level goals to the point where individual goals are spawned.

I recommend you share your goals with your advisory board to bring accountability and to benefit from their experiences and remarks. To do lists should be established, tracked, and checked for alignment with the stated goals.

Desired Actions or Goals I Will Take from Pointer 3

1. _____

_____

2. _____

_____

3. _____

_____

If you do everything that everyone else does in business, you're
going to lose. The only way to really be ahead, is to be different.
– Larry Ellison

The Difference Between an Entrepreneur and a Worker

N ow ask yourself if you can distinguish between an entrepreneur and a worker. Go beyond the obvious: that an entrepreneur generally owns the business while the worker works in the business and is hired by the entrepreneur.

I was posed that question by an entrepreneur on a flight from Detroit to Los Angeles. My immediate response was that entrepreneurs have a vested interest in the success of their business and will do whatever is required to meet the needs of the organization. Workers, on the other hand, no matter how conscientious, are limited in their willingness and ability to freely do what is necessary for the organization.

Most entrepreneurs are not confined by risks; they see the dangers or obstacles in front of them but are adept in finding solutions that allow them to move forward toward their goals. They are visionaries who act on their hypotheses and make changes when their ideas fail. Workers see risks as not their responsibility.

Successful companies have learned to empower their employees to think, test, and offer ideas to move the company forward; in effect, create an entrepreneurial spirit. Past examples from my experiences include Hughes Aircraft Company and Rockwell International, Haagen-Dazs, Amazon, Mattel, Google, Georgia Pacific, Raytheon, and Northrop Grumman.

Desired Actions or Goals I Will Take from Pointer 4

1. _____

   _____

2. _____

   _____

3. _____

   _____

It is better to look ahead and prepare
than to look back and regret.
– Jackie Joyner-Kersee

Be an Employee of Your Company

I have spoken with numerous small business owners who have not set themselves up as employees of their company. This is not as important for sole proprietors but a must for partnerships and corporations. We are all getting older, no matter at what age you start your enterprise. Whether or not you believe that Social Security will be available when you reach retirement age, currently it still is in existence. So why not plan for it? To secure Social Security you must pay FICA taxes. These taxes are automatically taken out of each of your employees' checks as payroll taxes. As an employee, your payroll checks would also be subjected to payroll taxes and you will receive a W-2 at the beginning of each year.

Employees have benefits, and as an employee, you can enjoy the benefits of being an owner and an employee. You become more conscious to pay yourself at regular pay periods. You can also be included on worker's compensation insurance (which I highly recommend), are more apt to schedule vacations (time off) and can participate in health care plans. You are also eligible for state disability insurance.

Time flies and when you look up, as I have, thirty-plus years have gone by. I have been an employee of my company during the entire period. I am eligible for Social Security, have participated in my company's 401(k) plan, and look forward to regular pay periods.

Desired Actions or Goals I Will Take from Pointer 5

1. _____

_____

2. _____

_____

3. _____

_____

Everyone has been made for some particular work, and
the desire for that work has been put in every heart.
- Rumi

Hire the Skill Set, Not the Person

Your enterprise is evolving, and it is time to hire employees. The biggest tip I can give you is to determine the skill set required for the positions you are planning to fill (strong analytical prowess, programming or software knowledge, a sales closer, supervisory experience, etc.). Create job descriptions and interview questions and focus on these during the interview process. Liking the person is important but secondary. Take the time to check references to glean validation that the candidate has demonstrated the skill set you desire. Ask the hard questions. For example, if someone is applying for a position as a mechanical engineer knowledgeable about SOLIDWORKS you may ask questions like, How do we get a square hole? Can you tell me the different types of hardware (screws, thread pitches, materials, etc.) that can be used and why you would choose one over the other? Ask the candidate to demonstrate their skill set. In the previous example, ask the candidate to sit in front of a Solidworks computer and navigate the Solidworks software. Their ease of use and familiarity will be quickly exposed; it's hard to fake experience using a tool or software.

Now here is MY Achilles heel! I see value in all persons and have hired individuals because I believed they could learn to do the job that was required. In many instances I was disappointed. Applicants are excellent at interviewing but once hired many do not demonstrate the same level of knowledge or commitment as expressed during the interview process once they become part of your work force. If you focus intently on the skill set you require during the interview process, you can better select the right person for the position.

Desired Actions or Goals I Will Take from Pointer 6

1. _____

_____

2. _____

_____

3. _____

_____

Tread Very Lightly When Hiring Friends:
They May Prove Difficult to Manage

As an entrepreneur, you have an idea of the culture you want your organization to have. In the infancy stage, when capital to grow the business may be limited, we may choose to rely on friends to assist in moving the business along. You share your business venture idea with some friends, and a few take an interest in helping you succeed. In the beginning their assistance may be beneficial, but as the business starts to grow additional people, skill sets and wage requirements creep into the mix. It may be difficult to make those decisions that are best for the business if your friends are your employees. How do you tell your friends that you expect increased productivity, that you are hiring someone who will be their supervisor, or that you simply no longer require their services? What is the perception of your non-friend employees of your relationship with your employee friends? What effect is this having on your business culture, on your ability to manage, and your decision-making? Are you more apt to bend company policies because the employee is your friend? The use of friends within your enterprise may be necessary at times; however, be aware of the risks and limitations imposed by hiring friends.

Desired Actions or Goals I Will Take from Pointer 7

1. _____

_____

2. _____

_____

3. _____

_____

I noticed there was nothing in the employee handbook
about snacks, naps, or pet's birthdays.
— E.J. Pettinger

The Employee Handbook:
The Most Relied Upon Corporate Document

Outside of a partnership agreement or corporate by-laws, the Employee Handbook should be one of the initial policy documents created for your business. It should be in existence before hiring your first employee. There are many templates available online so creating one is not difficult, however, take heed, for templates are just that. You must tailor the template to your specific corporate culture. Remember, employee manuals are not static documents. They must be updated regularly as employment laws change frequently and may vary from state-to-state.

Why this emphasis on having an Employee Handbook or manual? Simply for clarity; it removes or addresses any ambiguities relating to handling of employees. It clearly defines employee benefits (health plan; savings plan, including corporate matching; sick and vacation days with calculations; payroll periods; holidays; maternity/paternity leave, etc.) and distinguishes between full-time, part-time and contract labor.

The Employee Handbook includes your discrimination policy and rules of conduct to be followed at your company. Conflict of interest and employee invention agreements are also included. Disciplinary actions for misconduct, including termination, should be defined within the Employee Handbook. It is recommended that a copy of the handbook be given to each employee on the first day of their employment. A signature indicating receipt should be maintained within their employee file.

Many times, over the course of managing my team, there have been questions on whether we celebrate a specific holiday or what happens if the holiday falls on a Saturday or Sunday. In these instances, we always refer to our Employee Handbook for clarity. I had one experience where an employee whom we had terminated went to the labor board to sue for underpayment of final wages. The judge who presided over the case asked if we had an Employee Handbook and, if yes, wanted to see a copy of it. We were able to prevail in this case because the issue in dispute was clearly addressed in our Employee Handbook. The judge did suggest a change that we could make to our handbook that would eliminate the issue from becoming one in the future. We updated our handbook on the next revision and made all employees aware of the revised document. We received signed notifications of receipt from each employee and added them to their employee files.

Desired Actions or Goals I Will Take from Pointer 8

1. _____

_____

2. _____

_____

3. _____

_____

Cut Out Cancer Early

I am referring to cancerous employees – those employees who feed off negativity and who do not speak or act in the best light of the organization. They are individuals who undermine the direction of supervision and management, complain about the organization, and try to rally other employees around their negativity. They create discord in your organization and need to be removed. So, cut the cancer out early to prevent spreading!

I have had employees in sales complain about their sales quotas and act in ways detrimental to the future of our company. Hence, their employment was terminated. We experienced engineering personnel who sidestepped our quality requirements and falsely accused our vendors. They were also removed from their position. We also experienced production personnel who would not follow workstation instructions, who relied on knowledge of past actions to dictate how they processed current jobs, and who complained to other employees when they are reprimanded. These are the same employees who would take all their vacation and sick time, leave promptly when their shift ended, and needed to be reminded that personal cell phone use is not allowed during work hours. They do not represent the characteristics of preferred employees for our company and they, too, had to be replaced.

The point is that once you see that employees are not working in the best interest of the organization; they should be replaced. With all the responsibilities of running the organization, you may have the tendency to allow employee-related issues to manifest. Employees are the backbone of the organization and having the right mix of employees is critical to the success of the company. One bad apple can spoil the bunch so remove the bad one and allow the bunch to blossom. The sooner, the better.

When planning on terminating employees, check with labor attorneys and human resource consultants to learn the proper steps to take to avoid legal repercussions. Labor laws vary from state-to-state so verify in advance that your planned actions are in accordance with the applicable state's labor laws. Handling troublesome employees should be discussed with your advisory board.

Desired Actions or Goals I Will Take from Pointer 9

1. _____

_____

2. _____

_____

3. _____

_____

There is only one boss. The customer. And he can fire
everybody in the company from the chairman on down,
simply by spending his money somewhere else.
- Sam Walton

Sales: *The Life Blood of Any Organization*

There were two adages that stuck in my mind as an inspiring entrepreneur. First, the sales team is the most important group within your organization and second, you cannot screw up an order that you do not have. Your company can have the best engineers, software developers, production team, and most sophisticated capital equipment, but if there are no sales coming in then your business will falter.

In the infancy stage of a business, the entrepreneur is usually functioning in the role as the salesperson. The problem is that most entrepreneurs are not salespeople and do not know how to build a successful sales team, however, they can be excellent closers because customers feel the passion and commitment of the founder and are moved to trust the entrepreneur.

I have heard many definitions of the sales function but none better than the one my father lives by, "Sales or selling is the art of causing another to think, feel, and act according to your preconceived idea."

Salespeople are a unique bunch. I have heard repeatedly from successful salespersons that sales are about creating and maintaining relationships and when it comes to servicing customers, one size does not fit all. You must meet prospective and existing customers where they are and move them to take the action you desire, which in most cases is the issuance of a purchase order or ordering your products and services. Successful sales employees generally will be the highest paid individuals in your company, even higher than the CEO or founder. Some entrepreneurs have difficulty with this, however, a word of caution when setting up commission structures for your sales personnel. Try not to limit the amount of commissions a salesperson can earn. Quality salespersons are motivated by compensation. Limiting their achievable compensation can have a negative effect on your business.

Sales are the responsibility of <u>everyone</u> in your organization, not just the salesperson. Key responsibilities: knowing standard operating procedures throughout the different organizational functions; focusing on high quality, low rework; meeting delivery commitments; providing sales order status to the sales person in a timely manner so they can keep the customer informed; maintaining a neat and orderly facility; implementing a continuous improvement program and aiming to always "Wow" your customers. These are just some of the ways members of your organization can support their sales team. At our company, all departments understand that they exist to support the sales team.

Your sales team will need an operating budget. We have all heard, "It takes money to make money," and this holds true in most sales organizations. Salespeople need to know that there are funds available to nurture relationships with their clients and perspective clients in a manner suitable for the opportunity. Travel, meals and entertainment, mileage, samples, shipping, and training are just some of the costs that salespersons may incur.

Desired Actions or Goals I Will Take from Pointer 10

1. _____

   _____

2. _____

   _____

3. _____

   _____

*It's okay to have all of your eggs in one basket as long
as you control what happens to that basket.*
– Elon Musk

The Partnership Agreement:
A Must at the Beginning of the Enterprise

Friends may get together and decide that they have an idea for a venture they could launch. Excitement flares at the potential of this venture truly taking off. Before getting too engulfed in pursuing the idea, it is important that a Partnership Agreement be prepared that delineates the role of each partner within the new enterprise. Word of mouth, a trusting handshake, and family association are good to have, but never in lieu of a signed partnership agreement. There are several partnership agreement templates available online. Once one is selected it will walk you through identifying:

a. How are decisions made?
b. When and how are wages paid to the partners?
c. What are the capital infusion requirements of each partner and the corresponding share of ownership?
d. What is the procedure for a partner to leave the enterprise? In many cases, a right of first refusal for the partner's stock ownership is identified.
e. What are the roles, titles, and responsibilities of each partner?

The Partnership Agreement should be treated as a legal document. In the event of a partner dispute, the Partnership Agreement can be a major source for final determination. Do not take this agreement lightly. For ventures starting as a corporation, the Partnership Agreement is your By-Laws.

When we first started JET, there were three partners. I had a mentor who owned a successful materials supply company that serviced the electronics industry. I told him about the venture that we were starting and his first question to me was, "How many partners do you have?" My answer was three and his response was, "Two too many!" Later, when one of the partners sold his ownership back to the company, I told this mentor what had transpired, and his response was, "Still, one too many partners." Over the years I learned why he was so adamant about reducing the number of partners. Usually, there is one person who has the vision of how they want to take advantage of an opportunity. Others may see the opportunity but are not clear on the vision or the steps to act on the vision. The more partners presiding over a business entity the harder it is to follow a single vision. Successful partnerships allow the visionary to lead while the other partners support. The visionary is generally the entrepreneur who had the vision to start the enterprise. The position they hold within the company may not be the CEO or President.

Desired Actions or Goals I Will Take from Pointer 11

1. _____

   _____

2. _____

   _____

3. _____

   _____

With great power comes great responsibility.
— Stan Lee

Don't be Eager to be a Signer on Your Company's Checks

In smaller companies the entrepreneur signs the business checks; however, as the business grows, and a finance manager is hired, he/she may be authorized to sign the business checks. Did you know that signers of business checks can be held personally liable for business debt? There are times, such as in the case of unpaid payroll tax liabilities, when government agencies can even pierce the corporate veil to hold corporate officers and signers of corporate checks personally liable for unpaid corporate debt. It is for that reason that you should think twice about being a signer on business checks. When determining who had the authority to allocate business funds, interested parties will request copies of processed checks to determine the signer.

My recommendation is that there should only be one authorized signer of company checks, and if that person is unavailable to sign checks, have a signature stamp of that individual which can be used in an emergency. If you are an authorized signer for a small company, have the entrepreneur sign the payroll and tax related checks. This action may relieve you of payroll tax responsibility.

When first setting up your business, there may be discussions on having two persons sign checks over a specific amount. Ask your bank if they honor the two-signature requirement on corporate checks. I have found that many banks are only looking for one authorized signature on checks that are deposited. Thus, requiring dual signatures is more for internal corporate security versus external bank verification and can be a false sense of security.

Desired Actions or Goals I Will Take from Pointer 12

1. _____

   _____

2. _____

   _____

3. _____

   _____

To contract new debts is not the way to pay old ones.
— George Washington

The Importance of Good Business and Personal Credit

The cost of capital in support of your business is directly related to your business and personal credit score. Dun & Bradstreet will maintain a commercial credit score and financial stress class for your business. These scores are based on how well your business is paying its bills. To learn more about Dun & Bradstreet, go to www.dnp.com. Your vendors may be reporting your payment history to business credit bureaus: D&B, Experian, and Equifax. Most lenders will check your credit scores to determine your credit worthiness before agreeing to lines of credit and will use this information to assign an interest rate for cost of capital.

When I started JET, I had good credit and was able to obtain several credit cards. I was unable to get a line of credit from a bank due to my unwillingness to put my home up as collateral. As a business owner I operated under the philosophy that I would not tie my personal or family assets to my business. I wanted to get JET to the point where it could stand on its own. In my company's infancy, I used credit cards to finance much of my business. The more I borrowed and paid on time the more I was rewarded with higher credit limits.

Establishing a habit of paying your bills on a target date before they are due can be a very prudent policy for your company and can reap benefits. Your vendors will become conditioned to the fact that you pay your bills in this manner and will treat you as a preferred vendor. You will find it easier to obtain vendor references when requesting credit terms from new vendors. I have found that new vendors request referrals from at least three of your existing vendors to evaluate your credit history before granting payment terms.

Desired Actions or Goals I Will Take from Pointer 13

1. _____

   _____

2. _____

   _____

3. _____

   _____

Beware of little expenses. A small leak will sink a great ship.
— Benjamin Franklin

Your Shipping Motto: *Free Takes Awhile*

I f your new venture requires you to ship products to your customers, then you need to be aware of your shipping costs. These costs can easily get out of control. New prospects may request free samples or promotions of your products. Using shipping carriers, such as FedEx, UPS, or DHL are expensive, especially when selecting next day or two-day shipping. Uncontrollable shipping charges can also have an adverse effect on your cash flow since many of the shipping companies require automatic payment tied to a debit or credit card or linked to a business checking account. Shipping costs need to be monitored and controlled, and a shipping policy should be implemented to control them.

One way to control your shipping costs is to implement a strategy of "Free Takes A While." When offering to freely ship products or samples to customers, your policy should be the lowest shipping cost possible regardless of the shipping duration, that is, USPS standard rate. You can offer faster shipment; however, customers should pay for this service. When shipping B2B, you can request their UPS or Fed-Ex account and ship recipient collect. If shipping to a personal residence, you can give the option of adding the cost for faster shipment to the total cost of the order (prepay and add).

Desired Actions or Goals I Will Take from Pointer 14

1. _____

_____

2. _____

_____

3. _____

_____

Marketing without data is like driving with your eyes closed.
– Dan Zarrella

Test Your Market Before You Decide to Hang Your Shingle

Entrepreneurs are generally overly optimistic people. They believe that they can market their product or service because they are solving a problem. This is all well and good, but until it has been tested it is only a hypothesis. A test market strategy should be defined and implemented. There are many articles online on how to conduct a test market. The intent here is not to identify how to perform a test market, but to stress the importance of having proof, confirmation that you should move on marketing your product or service.

Prior to launching JET, I maintained a small company, Ford & Associates, to handle consulting opportunities. Under the auspices of Ford & Associates, I performed a test market by sending out questionnaires to process engineers at various hybrid facilities around the country. I primarily asked if they were manually marking their parts and would be interested in a digital marking system. I received a 21 percent response, and each response showed a 100 percent interest in a computer-controlled inkjet parts marking system.

If correctly done, the results of your test market will identify the initial customers who you should target. It will help to develop the customer characteristic definition and market segmentation. Without performing a test market, you are aiming blindly, spending company resources in an unfocused manner to attract prospective customers.

Desired Actions or Goals I Will Take from Pointer 15

1. _____

_____

2. _____

_____

3. _____

_____

The longer you hang in there, the greater the chance that
something will happen in your favor. No matter how hard it
seems, the longer you persist, the more likely your success.
– Jack Canfield

The Power of Persistence:
Keep Your Eyes on the Prize

Persistence is a character trait demonstrated by the ability to continue to get up no matter how many times you've been knocked down or failed. It requires will power, flexibility, strength of character, determination, and a desire to succeed at all costs.

If you have performed your test market and are confident that there is a viable market for your product or service, then I encourage you to set a goal – one that is tangible and measurable – and go for it. I set a goal for myself from the onset of JET's creation. My test marketing and future industry analysis confirmed that I should be able to achieve my goal. If I hadn't met my goal, then I was committed to persist until I did. Are YOU willing to persist until you DO?

I must caution that you will get many onlookers, possibly family members or friends, who don't understand your persistent nature and may encourage you to give up and get a job. But your employees believe in you, and most important, you believe in you. If you persist, you have a chance to reach your goal but if you quit, the game is over, and the goal cannot be reached.

I think it was Will Smith, the actor, who said, "You must set your goals so high that you must evolve to achieve them." If you are not reaching the goals that you have set for your enterprise then it may be that your company must evolve, and that you may have to evolve in order to achieve them. Are you willing to continue learning new business concepts, hire different skill sets, let go and let grow, hire your weaknesses, and train your strengths, or do those things necessary to evolve and reach your goals?

Desired Actions or Goals I Will Take from Pointer 16

1. _____

   _____

2. _____

   _____

3. _____

   _____

Pain Results in Change:
Feel the Pain and Move Forward

I credit Tony Robbins for helping me to make the attitude change necessary for me to leave my comfortable position at Hughes Aircraft Company and to pursue an entrepreneurial venture. I had to associate "pain" with going to Hughes every day and performing the tasks that at one point I had enjoyed. As that pain intensified, I began to move closer and closer to starting my own company. Learn to associate pain with the status quo when change is required.

As your enterprise experiences growing pains and you find that changes are needed but you are having a difficult time making those changes, I encourage you to associate pain with the current AS-IS scenario. That pain will cause you to move forward to a TO-BE realm, one where your goals and desires are met. For example, you may want to make organizational changes that will impact a long-term employee. This employee has shown loyalty over the years but is incapable of learning the new tools or processes that you are attempting to implement. If you associate pain with not being able to make the organizational changes that will take the organization in your desired direction, it may be easier for you to come to a win-win solution for you and the employee.

Over time, in the life of your enterprise, you will be faced with difficult situations, unplanned negative events or disgruntled customers. Acknowledge each existence, feel the pain, and now take positive steps to change the situation or your attitude towards the situation. Always take steps to move forward to a positive state where you are no longer dwelling on the negative.

Desired Actions or Goals I Will Take from Pointer 17

1. _____

   _____

2. _____

   _____

3. _____

   _____

If you can dream it, you can do it.
- Walt Disney

Visualize to Manifestation:
If You Can See It, You Can Achieve It

D o you see yourself running your own business, leading a team, or having a board meeting? If you can see it, then you can make it happen. Over the years I have used visualization techniques to move to a larger facility, to hire additional skill sets of employees, to improve vendor or customer relationships, to let go and let grow, or to reach a desired pay scale.

You are capable of manifesting anything you desire within your business, but first you must see it. It must appear real in your mind so that you can take the necessary steps to bring it to fruition. The real power comes when you have others in the organization see what you see and now they are onboard to make it happen. Want to reach new market segments or acquire competitive companies? Visualize it happening and then strategize to manifestation.

Some of the approaches that I have used to visualize a new product, enhance teamwork, seek new business opportunities, increase profit margins, meet payroll obligations, and so forth, are to:

Sit quietly and allow thoughts regarding my interest to appear – My goal is to obtain a clear mental picture of what I desire.

Assess, with honesty, where I or the organization is towards achieving the desire mental picture. Basically, answering the question, "What is stopping this from materializing? What must change?"

Plan, identify each step that needs to be taken to achieve my goal.

Pray, chant "nam myoho renge kyo" whenever possible to spiritually connect with my goal.

See myself achieving, doing, having what I visualized.

Desired Actions or Goals I Will Take from Pointer 18

1. _____

_____

2. _____

_____

3. _____

_____

A culture of accountability makes a good organization
great and a great organization unstoppable.
– Henry Evans

Entrepreneurship: *I Thought I Was the Boss*

When you ask aspiring entrepreneurs why they want to own their own businesses, the most common response is that they want to be their own boss. They want to be the person making the decisions versus being told what to do. So, do entrepreneurs have a boss? Absolutely! Entrepreneurs are accountable to their customers, shareholders, financers, advisory board, federal, state and city municipalities, tax boards, and creditors.

As an entrepreneur, you are the head of your enterprise. You have the power and authority to have the final say and to make the final decision. But do you want to across the board? Experienced entrepreneurs empower their people to make decisions on behalf of the enterprise. They want to focus more on growing their business versus working in their business; however, unless the entrepreneur has trained the staff to effectively address low and mid-level decisions, the entrepreneur can find themselves making decisions that should be made by their staff. Successful entrepreneurs are shielded from making sustaining-related decisions and can focus more on making growth and earnings decisions for the organization.

Desired Actions or Goals I Will Take from Pointer 19

1. _____

   _____

2. _____

   _____

3. _____

   _____

The goal isn't to get rid of all your negative thoughts and feelings; that's impossible. The goal is to change your response to them.
— Anonymous

I Hear a Symphony:
Channeling Negative Chatter

I have learned that the mind is immensely powerful and the thoughts that I allow to resonate do manifest. Simply stated, what I think about becomes a reality. As an entrepreneur there are negative thoughts that appear from time to time due to fear, conscious or subconscious awareness, or unsureness. These negative thoughts can place us in a state of paralysis or defensiveness as they tend to block the positive thoughts that are attempting to emerge. It is as though a symphony of doubt is being played within our head, and what is scary, is that we are beginning to listen!

How do I break this thought process? I channel these thoughts toward my goal. I ask myself, how are these thoughts helping me to move forward toward my goal? My mind quickly infers that they are not. Immediately, these negative thoughts begin to lose their power. The symphony is disbanding. I now can begin to visualize the manifestation, the result that I desire to achieve. Negative thoughts become powerless and are replaced with ideas, positive thoughts, on how I can take steps that will move me forward. My mind becomes clear and I am eager to take action.

How many times has the symphony of negative chatter been playing in your ear as you prepared to embark on your entrepreneurial journey? Here is the key: You don't try to stop the chatter. Instead, focus on your goal and allow the light of positive thoughts to continue to overshadow the negative symphony. Keeping your focus on the light and the possibilities of achieving your goal can dissipate your awareness of the negative chatter until at one point it is simply non-existent.

Desired Actions or Goals I Will Take from Pointer 20

1. _____

   _____

2. _____

   _____

3. _____

   _____

Nothing in life is to be feared. It is only to be understood.
— Marie Curie

Overcoming FEAR

Entrepreneurs are known as financial risk takers, so it is safe to assume that we also become fearful at times. How we handle fear varies from entrepreneur to entrepreneur. Whenever I become fearful about a situation that is occurring or an expectation of what I may be facing, I stop and remind myself of the FEAR acronym – FALSE EXPECTATIONS APPEARING REAL. I am reminded that most outcomes never match what I have created in my mind through fear. It is at these times that I may consult with my advisory board, a fellow entrepreneur, or anyone who can help me to see past my stifling concerns. I may refer to a situation that one of my role models overcame and use the strength of that situation to help me move forward.

Fear occurs when we perceive that something uncontrollable or unavoidable is going to happen. It hasn't happened yet, so therefore it exists only within our minds. We become so focused on what we don't want that we fail to give energy to the possibility of what we do want. I experienced an IRS problem that had me overcome with fear that the IRS was going to shut down my business. My fear was reinforced by an employee telling me that in his last position the IRS came to the business and padlocked the door. I had run all these negative scenarios in my mind until I spoke to a friend who told me that there are companies that specialize in helping with tax-related problems. I called several tax consultants and contracted with one who helped me work through my situation. I found the IRS to be helpful and willing to work with me, providing I submitted the information they requested in a timely manner, filed my returns on time, and worked to become compliant. None of the scenarios that I had feared became a reality.

Desired Actions or Goals I Will Take from Pointer 21

1. _____

   _____

2. _____

   _____

3. _____

   _____

The biggest mistake a small business can
make is to think like a small business.
– Anonymous

The Pros and Cons of Using a P.O. Box as the Primary Address

I strongly recommend the use of a P.O. Box address for your primary business mailing address. My personal preference is a box at your local post office; however, you may prefer to use a local mailbox center such as The UPS Store or a virtual mailbox. The Post Office Box mailing address is used on our business checks, credit card statements, invoices, and other business-related documents. The physical address is only used for receipt of purchased items. Wherever possible, choose a P.O. Box location that provides both a street address and P.O. Box address. Why? Because some business transactions require a physical address and will not accept a P.O. Box address. The use of a P.O. Box is ideal for home-based businesses, thereby keeping your actual home address anonymous.

There are a multitude of benefits in using a P.O. Box address for your business documents. Some of them include: no need to change all of your business documents (checks, invoices, bank statements, etc.) each time you physically move to a new location; provides better privacy and security for receipt of business documents; allows you to manage your business at your physical location without being taken aghast from something received in the mail; keeps junk mail from your physical location; affords you or your designate the opportunity to set time to retrieve the mail with intention; and if using a USPS box, you can address other mailing needs (procuring stamps, sending priority mail) while retrieving the mail. The use of a P.O.

Box address can allow the business to have a more desirable address versus your actual physical location.

The disadvantages of using a P.O. Box as your primary mailing address include: P.O. boxes are costly and need to be renewed periodically; they require travel to and from the P.O. Box to retrieve mail; they can be difficult to receive large items there; they require a key; and parking can be challenging at times.

Desired Actions or Goals I Will Take from Pointer 22

1. _____

   _____

2. _____

   _____

3. _____

   _____

In business -- every business -- the bottom line is
understanding the process. If you don't understand the
process, you'll never reap the rewards of the process.
– Donald Trump

Last Paper on File

When I first started JET, a good friend of mine, who was a buyer for a major aircraft manufacturer, explained to me the importance of understanding contract terms and conditions, as well as which company's legal documents would be binding during a transaction. For example, when we send a quotation for a JET marking system to a customer, we include our terms and conditions of sale. The company purchasing the equipment sends a purchase order with their terms and conditions on the backside or included as an addendum. In most cases, they will also request a signed acknowledgement of the purchase order. When we sign the acknowledgment copy, we are foregoing our terms and conditions and have agreed to theirs. The signed acknowledgment is the last paper on file and thus, the binding terms and conditions. Talk to your attorney if you wish for your terms to be binding. It may be as simple as signing the acknowledgement with a note that the attached terms and conditions of sale will be in effect.

Desired Actions or Goals I Will Take from Pointer 23

1. _____

   _____

2. _____

   _____

3. _____

   _____

Read carefully anything that requires your signature.
Remember, the big print giveth and the small print taketh away.
– H. Jackson Brown, Jr.

Take the Time to Read the Fine Print:
The Devil is in the Details

As an entrepreneur, you will be inundated with documents requiring signature. From lease agreements to customer/vendor terms and conditions, there is fine print that should be understood and accepted before signing. Make sure you understand what the document is actually saying and not what your optimistic attitude wants or thinks it is saying. I had a situation that occurred with our phone service. We had agreed to an introductory twelve-month rate with the understanding that after that period the rate would increase. My intention was to investigate alternatives before the end of the twelve-month period. What I failed to make note of was that within the agreement there was an automatic renewal clause if I did not notify them within thirty days from the end of the term that I would be terminating my agreement. The thirty-day period lapsed, I went into automatic renewal and when I called to cancel, I was informed that there would be a cost for what was now considered "early termination."

Should you decide to do factoring or obtain non-traditional [bank loan, line of credit] financing, be sure to read the fine print relating to additional charges, fees, or prepayment penalties. When signing up for services – cleaning, telephone, drinking water, payroll, manpower, and so on – read the fine print to be clear on the terms of the agreement and how to exit the service should you desire.

Regarding legal documents, avoid being penny wise and pound foolish. Pay to have experienced legal counsel review legal documents to make you aware of the ramifications that are disclosed within the fine print.

Desired Actions or Goals I Will Take from Pointer 24

1. _____

   _____

2. _____

   _____

3. _____

   _____

When Seeking Capital:
Double Your Financing Estimations

Cash flow is the life blood of a business. The lack of adequate cash hampers your ability to make timely decisions and to act on opportunities. Thus, when determining capital requirements to start a business or take on a new project, I recommend you at least double your estimation. No matter how detailed your financial projections are you cannot predict everything. There must be a financial buffer for unplanned expenses, mistakes, or changes. We tend to ask for just what we think we need when borrowing capital. The fallacy in this thought process is that if you don't have sufficient capital to meet your objective, then it will take that much longer for you to receive the desired effect and be in a position to pay back the loan. Ask for more, spend less, and payback sooner is a viable strategy.

Cash flow considerations include: payroll, payroll deposits, and payroll taxes; business liability and worker's compensation insurance; prepay and COD payments; professional services; utilities; capital equipment; travel expenses; and employee draws.

Desired Actions or Goals I Will Take from Pointer 25

1. _____

   _____

2. _____

   _____

3. _____

   _____

Planning is bringing the future into the present
so that you can do something about it now.
– Alan Lakein

Build Equity from the Start:
Plan Early to Own Your Building

I have been an entrepreneur for over 30 years and one of my regrets is that I did not take the required actions to own my facility. My advice to aspiring entrepreneurs and those who currently own a business is to set a goal to own your building. It is important to start as early as possible. You don't get the time back. I encourage you to start associating pain with paying rent. Each time you make a rent payment you should say to yourself this payment could be going towards ownership of my own building.

Owning your own facility affords you collateral when applying for a business loan. You have an appreciating asset versus a monthly liability. Check with your accountant to see how owning your facility may provide tax benefits and significantly improve your balance sheet. Are you planning on selling your business at some point? You could sell the business, hold on to the real estate, and then lease the space to the acquiring company.

The company that has successfully implemented this strategy is McDonald's Corporation. McDonald's sells burgers and fries to buy real estate. The profit from their real estate holdings far exceeds that from selling their menu items. They are one of the largest real estate owners worldwide. As Ray Kroc would say, "My business is real estate. We sell French fries to purchase real estate."

On a smaller scale, I have a vendor who has owned his machine shop business for over thirty-five years. Recently he got frustrated about the current business cycle and the slow payment of his vendors. He informed me that he was offered $2.5 million dollars for his building that he owns free and clear. He learned at an early age of running his business the importance of owning his facility.

Desired Actions or Goals I Will Take from Pointer 26

1. _____

_____

2. _____

_____

3. _____

_____

In any moment of decision, the best thing you can do
is the right thing, the next thing is the wrong thing,
and the worst thing you can do is nothing.
– Theodore Roosevelt

Pay Your Taxes on Time

What's just as constant as the sun rising and falling daily, can accrue exorbitant penalties and interest if not paid on time, and can cause you to be its steward? Business Taxes.

Businesses are responsible for collecting and paying taxes on a regularly scheduled basis. For example, payroll taxes are due after each scheduled payroll distribution; sales tax collected is paid quarterly and/or annually depending on your filing status; property taxes are paid annually, as well as earnings (profits).

Paying taxes on time has been my Achilles heel, my nemesis. It is not that I don't understand the importance of paying my business taxes on time; it is just that cash flow can be sporadic for a capital equipment business. What I have learned is that you must plan payment of your taxes before they are due. They must be factored into your cash disbursements and set aside as they are received. It is advisable to have a separate bank account for the accumulation of funds for payment of tax liabilities. As the head of your enterprise, you should be knowledgeable of your business tax obligations.

Should you ever fall behind, unable to pay your tax obligations, remember to always file your returns on time, even if no payment can be sent. There are stiff penalties for failing to file your returns. Contact your tax agency and ask to get on a payment plan. Most tax agencies will work with you to resolve your tax debt. Under no circumstance should you run and hide or avoid the numerous notices sent your way. Tax debt does not just go away, it will only get worse. Remember, inaction is action but an unwise choice. Talk with your advisory board and get the company the tax help it needs.

Desired Actions or Goals I Will Take from Pointer 27

1. _____

   _____

2. _____

   _____

3. _____

   _____

There is never a perfect time to start. "And if you start six months from now, you will wish you started six months earlier. If you start tomorrow, you will wish you started yesterday."
— Samantha Ettus

Pay Yourself First

Your employees are the most valuable assets of your organization. As the business owner you are focused on making sure your employees are taken care of first; however, unless you view yourself also as an employee there exists a tendency to pay yourself last. I strongly recommend that you get into the habit of paying yourself first. Rid yourself of the attitude that you will wait until the company is doing better before you pay yourself. You will find it much easier to maintain that home/work financial balance, especially if you have a spouse. Financial problems in your home life can exist if you are not bringing home a regular, predictable paycheck.

Set a minimum amount that you *must* pay yourself, no matter how small. For example, say your goal is to achieve an annual salary of $100,000 but your erratic cash flow does not support you taking $8,333.33 per month. It does however support $50,000 annually or $4,166.67 per month. Put yourself on a minimum payroll amount and increase that amount randomly as the business cash flow permits. You can also create an arrears account whereby the business is keeping track of your unpaid earnings. This arrears account should be reviewed quarterly, semi-annually, or annually to determine how much it can be reduced based on cash availability.

I have found that getting a paycheck, no matter how small, on payday, along with the rest of the employees, strengthens my view of the team <u>and</u> provides a consistent metric on how the business is performing. Psychologically, I found myself more focused on getting the team better trained and more productive because the net result was improved cash flow and a ramping of my personal salary. In addition, those periods where I was not getting paid, but my employees were, created a sense of resentment or negativity towards employees who were not performing to the best of their abilities but were always present on pay day. By including myself as part of payroll, I felt more part of the team and was able to convey my observations and expectations without resentment.

Desired Actions or Goals I Will Take from Pointer 28

1. _____

   _____

2. _____

   _____

3. _____

   _____

How bad do you want it?
— Eric Thomas

Not Every Deal Is the Right One for Your Company

You just hung your shingle or created your online presence, and you are ready to satisfy your customers. Prospective clients are showing interest in your products and services while at the same time you are conscious of the monthly costs to stay in business. You have a clear idea of your pricing structure, the market segment, and the characteristics of the preferred customer, but you are feeling pressured to show or increase sales revenues. You are ripe to take your enterprise down a spiraling detour from your business plan. One of the actions you may take is to decrease your price to the breakeven point or worse, below, to get the order. (I will admit that there are times when this strategy is an effective one, for example, to gain entry in a market or company where, in the future, it can lead to additional sales or higher profit margins. But it must be a conscious decision.) You might decide to take an order that deviates from your current market strategy or requires modification to your standard product that cannot be sold to other customers or is in a market that your company has decided is not a target market. There are always justifications for why you ponder taking an order that is not in accordance with your strategic plan. The question you must ask yourself is: If we take this order, what opportunities are we not able to respond to because of the resource demand to satisfy this order? Have we looked at the true opportunity cost risks?

As an equipment manufacturer we have been a victim of order diversion to the point where it seemed we were a custom equipment company versus one selling standard products. Each time we said "yes" to a prospective customer's request that deviated from our standard products we had to spend more engineering time, additional training and introducing more confusion to our manufacturing team. One time I was discussing this phenomenon with a fellow business owner and he said, "Not all deals are good deals for your company." He went on to say, "A bad deal going in never gets better." Those words of wisdom stayed on my mind and I continually remind my team of those points.

You want to grow your business, be innovative in satisfying your customer's wants, desires, and needs, while at the same time protect your company from splintering into various directions. Monitor and resist the degree of customization of orders and strive for standardization. Give the customers what they want in the realm of your standard capabilities and, if you must deviate, charge for the changes being offered.

Desired Actions or Goals I Will Take from Pointer 29

1. _____

   _____

2. _____

   _____

3. _____

   _____

The more clear you are about what you want, the more motivated and determined you will be to accomplish it.
– Brian Tracy

Know Your Core Values:
Remind Yourself of What's Important to You

Inevitably you are going to have difficult times being an entrepreneur. There may be times when the thought arises to quit and to get a steady day job. You will have those days where it seems you are going backwards, not making progress. You may be plagued with financial, employee, legal, tax matters, or management issues to the point where your frustration level regarding your business has peaked. On the other hand, problems at home with your spouse, children, or elderly relatives may add stress that is causing you to be ineffective at work. It is during these times that clearly knowing what is important to you can help you move toward the right action.

There are only twenty-four hours in a day. Your business, your family and taking care of yourself, demand a portion of these hours daily. Knowing your core values is essential to your time management and decision-making processes. If your relationship with your family is important, then you will attempt to schedule your time to be present for key events that are important to them. If succeeding against odds or challenges is one of your core values, then you will view business challenges as opportunities to learn and evolve as a business owner versus the ever-increasing internal stress that is deflating and defeating you. Challenges are opportunities for you to grow in resolve and resiliency.

Over the years, I been through several recessions that seriously impacted capital equipment manufacturers, forcing many to quit and go out of business. I have faced 1120 and 941 tax problems (which are two of the most serious IRS tax problems for a business owner), had key employees leave without replacements, experienced international copying of our technology, and seen competition emerge within our target markets. Through all these situations, I maintained a strong belief in myself, my business, the products and services we rendered, and that I would prevail.

Desired Actions or Goals I Will Take from Pointer 30

1. _____

    _____

2. _____

    _____

3. _____

    _____

Manage the process, not the people.
- Joe Apfelbaum

Let Go and Let's Grow

My advice to business owners is to hire and train a competent team, clearly express the goals and objectives of the organization, provide the necessary resources, and then "Get Out of The Way." Let your team demonstrate their ability to do what is required to meet the goals that have been defined. Understand that mistakes will be made, and if they take responsibility and learn from their mistakes, the organization will continue to grow. The key is not to become a micromanager to the point where everything is flowing through you. You become the bottleneck of your business. Your team becomes paralyzed when making decisions on behalf of the business.

Over the years, I have been guilty of micromanaging under the guise of learning all aspects of my business. Yes, it important for entrepreneurs to understand their business and the critical tasks required to keep the business afloat; however, if you, instead of a member of your team, are answering to customers on behalf of your organization, then this is an indication that you have not let go and let grow. If members of your organization are giving ideas in their areas of responsibility on how to address business concerns (design plans, software features, manufacturing procedures, HR policies) and you are interceding or shutting them down to have it done your way, then you may be limiting your enterprise from growing.

One technique that I used to reduce my micromanaging behaviors was to become more conscious of how much time I was spending daily working *in* my business versus *on* the business. With this clarity I was able to empower my team to manage and sustain the business while I worked more on growing the business.

Now ask yourself: Are you listening to the advice of your advisory board and hired consultants or are you still trying to do it your way first? The natural behavior of entrepreneurs is to believe in their own thoughts and ideas. When given contradicting information from known experts we still want to test our ideas first. In some cases, we act prudently and get a second opinion but once the differing information has been confirmed, we still want to hold on to our beliefs and ideas. When we act in this manner, we are hurting our enterprise. It is during these times we need to trust. Let go and let grow.

Desired Actions or Goals I Will Take from Pointer 31

1. _____

   _____

2. _____

   _____

3. _____

   _____

Attitude is Everything.
– Paul Meyer

Business Loans May Require Life Insurance:
Collateral Assignment

I t is common to expect banks and other sources of business loans to require some sort of collateral before entering into a loan agreement. Collateral are those assets that can be sold by the lender for cash and are viewed as a second source of loan repayment. Traditional assets include accounts receivables, machinery and equipment, buildings and, in some cases, inventory. Collateral can be in the form of business and/or personal assets.

My lender required a guarantee backed by a key life insurance policy on the principals of the business. We were required to obtain a life insurance policy in the amount of the loan, name the lender as the beneficiary and show periodically through the life of the loan that the insurance was still in effect.

It was an awkward feeling for me acquiring a life insurance policy and setting the beneficiary as the lender, someone outside of my immediate family. Maybe I watch too many movies, but I had to squash the thoughts that I could be at personal danger should I have difficulty meeting the terms of the loan. Instead, I focused on meeting my financial obligations and using the loan proceeds as planned.

Are you prepared to secure a personal life insurance policy to cover your business loan? You may be required to do so.

Desired Actions or Goals I Will Take from Pointer 32

1. _____

_____

2. _____

_____

3. _____

_____

Sustainability has to be a way of life to be a way of business.
— Anand Mahindra

Piercing the Corporate Veil

Many aspiring entrepreneurs choose the Corporation (S-Corp, C-Corp or LLC) as their preferred corporate structure to protect the owners, shareholders, directors, and members from being held personally liable for the company's debts or liabilities. I caution you to be aware that there are instances where the corporate veil can be pierced, and individuals can be held liable for the company's debts, liabilities, and actions. These instances include:

-   Negligence on the part of owners, directors, shareholders, and members.
-   A signer of the corporation's checks – signers are viewed as having control of which bills are paid and those which are not.
-   Falling into a suspended or forfeited status by state tax agencies for failure to meet tax obligations.
-   Engaging in wrongful or fraudulent behavior.
-   Failure to follow corporate formalities – holding annual meetings of directors and shareholders; keeping corporate minutes up to date; following corporate by-laws.
-   No clear separation between the corporation and its owners or members – *that is, commingling of personal and business assets.*
-   Under-capitalization – the corporation has inadequate or lacks access to adequate capital to operate. The corporation is unable to stand on its own.

- One person or a small group of closely related people have complete control of the corporation.

I have found that small companies have a harder time protecting against piercing of the corporate veil due to their size and habitual business practices. They lack the awareness, resources, focus, and fortitude to follow corporate formalities at the beginning of their incorporation, so as they grow, misaligned behaviors become part of their corporate culture. It would be advisable for corporations, regardless of size, to perform periodic corporate structure review audits.

Desired Actions or Goals I Will Take from Pointer 33

1. _____

   _____

2. _____

   _____

3. _____

   _____

Commit to finding the gift in any setback. Not only will you gain from each experience, but the combination of your commitment, courage, and faith will be the greatest triumph of all.
— Cynthia Kersey

Embrace Problems: *Learning is Forthcoming*

The world of an entrepreneur is for the most part dynamic. With dynamism come problems or challenges. When a serious unexpected problem occurs, our first response can be to freeze, to become paralyzed to act. We may seek to blame, to defer responsibility, or to overact in a manner that may hurt a relationship or the business in the long term.

Problems are opportunities presenting themselves. Over the years I had unexpected issues arise that were daunting, formidable, or downright alarming. Examples include: unauthorized funds withdrawn from our bank account; dealing with a bank's $888,888.88 withdrawal hold; tax levies; receipt of incorrect incoming supplier materials; loss of key employees; cash flow shortages at critical times; and insufficient supply to meet critical customer demands. These types of problems can be overwhelming and, if not handled correctly, can leave the organization faltering.

In each of the examples presented, as with most problems, there is something to be learned by the experience. Yes, it is difficult as you are going through the situations but by changing your attitude from **Why** or **How** is this happening to **What** can I do to get past this, you open yourself to infinite possibilities. For example, fraudulent checks have been debited from your account. In talking with the bank, you may improve or establish a relationship with someone there. In my case, I learned that we needed more secure checks that prohibit thieves from attempting to forge our business check. With tax levies, we were able to create a relationship with the tax agency and learn about the many programs available to deal with payment of delinquent taxes. Looking into the problem with incorrect incoming supplier materials, we learned that we had to implement better checks and balances during the ordering of materials and to have improved communications with our vendors on the status of our orders. In every case, we were able to solve the problem and learn how to implement policies and procedures to avoid these and like situations from occurring in the future. Learning can be painful, but it is necessary to run a successful and sustaining organization.

Desired Actions or Goals I Will Take from Pointer 34

1. _____

_____

2. _____

_____

3. _____

_____

The best six doctors anywhere, and no one can deny
it, are sunshine, water, rest, air, exercise, and diet.
– Wayne Fields

Eat & Drink Right to Stay Sharp

Entrepreneurship can be stressful at times and we all handle stress differently. If not careful, we may tend to create stress-induced habits – drinking too much caffeine, eating fast foods, missing meals, munching on sugary foods, and drinking insufficient water. We need our minds and our bodies to be sharp as we tackle the daily challenges. Taking in proper nutrition is the key to being mentally prepared to handle that which is brought before you.

Some tips on how to eat right and staying hydrated include: eating a balanced breakfast daily, placing a refrigerator in your office and stocking it with healthy foods, like fruits and vegetables, in addition to peanut butter and jam. Keeping a water bottle in your office and filling it up daily. You may want to make sure a water dispenser is nearby so that you will be more inclined to fill up regularly. Keep munchies like nuts, protein or power bars, or sunflower seeds readily available in a desk drawer or cabinet. Reduce with the intention of eliminating soda, including diet soda, from your diet. Sodas, candy bars, cookies and doughnuts contain high levels of sugar. Think of sugar and stress as being arch enemies. You can't always predict the level of stress you will encounter but you can control your sugar content. Too much of anything is not good for you and coffee falls into this category. If you are a heavy coffee drinker, you may want to set some goals to lower your consumption. You may try replacing the urge for coffee with tea or water. Finally, be mindful of your alcohol consumption. I attend many dinners, meetings, and gatherings where alcohol is served. I have become a master at making one drink last the event.

There are many references on eating right on the internet. You know if you are not eating properly. The challenge for you as an entrepreneur is to prepare your mind and body to lead your organization. It starts with you being as healthy as possible. Diet plays a vital role in determining your ability to handle stress.

Desired Actions or Goals I Will Take from Pointer 35

1. _____

   _____

2. _____

   _____

3. _____

   _____

Exercise not only changes your body, it changes
your mind, your attitude and your mood.
— Anonymous

The Importance of Physical Exercise

S leeping has never been a problem for me. One reason may be that I exercise frequently. From walking the dog daily, going to the gym, taking a few yoga classes (my new thing is aerial yoga), to playing basketball on the weekend, I prepare my body to be tired. As entrepreneurs we have a lot on our mind and many times, if the body is not tired, our overactive mind prevents us from getting a good night's sleep. One way to counteract this is to be physically tired.

Aside from sleeping better, being physically fit has other benefits. The cost for life insurance is far less expense for fit individuals. Physically fit individuals take less time off from work and are more capable of dealing with the daily stresses of entrepreneurship. Their immune systems are more robust and thus can better ward off germs or viruses when traveling or interacting with other individuals, especially employees. They generally look good and feel good about themselves, which leads to more of a positive aura and attitude.

Physically fit entrepreneurs also have other interest and thus maintain a better balance between being at work and away from work. Some of the common interests that I have seen entrepreneurs engage in include: handball, hiking, cycling, surfing, swimming, jogging, attending health spas/gyms and participating in club sports (basketball, baseball, soccer, and volleyball).

When I have a stressful day, I look forward to either going to the gym and working out, going on a cycling ride, or visiting the archery range. It seems that afterward, the stresses of the day dissipate, and I am ready to recharge my mind and body through sleep as I prepare for the next day.

Desired Actions or Goals I Will Take from Pointer 36

1. _____

   _____

2. _____

   _____

3. _____

   _____

Journal writing is a voyage to the interior.
— Christina Baldwin

The Power of Journaling

If you are not someone who journals regularly, then I strongly recommend that you consider it. You can purchase a hard-bound journal, or you can use your laptop or computer. I prefer to write daily in my journal versus using my digital device. A journal is your private tool to record your thoughts and feelings. Journaling allows me to empty my mind of present thoughts but know that they are being retained. It provides an opportunity for my conscious mind to learn what the unconscious mind has been thinking. When I record a problem I may have experienced, it appears that problem loses its weight. I am more mindful and now able to come up with viable solutions.

While journaling I can set personal and business goals and establish thought plans A, B, and C on how to achieve them. I am free to disclose feelings about partners, customers, employees, spouse, and children. Many times, honestly recording how I feel at the moment is freeing. It is my method of letting off steam without seriously damaging a relationship. In the movie *Shrek* there is a saying, "Better out than in." I believe this applies to our thoughts as well. Rather than continually rehash or analyze thoughts internally, when you write them down it seems you get a sense of clarity. You may find that you feel lighter after moving thoughts to paper and now have the capacity to bring in new thoughts for consideration.

I have been journaling since I started my business over thirty years ago. When I review some of my older journals, I can see areas or habits that have changed as well as those that have not. I can see how I evolved over time and some of the thoughts I had with limited information. What bothers me is when I see a habit that I have held on to over the years that has not been to my best interest. The good news is that now that I am mindful of it, I am open to changing it.

There are many health and healing benefits of journaling as well. I encourage you to research journaling and the many benefits. As an entrepreneur, you may find this activity to be priceless.

Desired Actions or Goals I Will Take from Pointer 37

1. _____

   _____

2. _____

   _____

3. _____

   _____

We all have dreams. But in order to make dreams
come into reality, it takes an awful lot of determination,
dedication, self-discipline, and effort.
– Jesse Owens

Hold on To Your Dream

When I started my business, I set a goal for myself. That goal was to become a ten million-dollar business, and I have not reached that goal. I have wanted to quit and pull the plug, but two things stopped me. First, I genuinely enjoy what I do and the products and services that our company offers. I take pleasure in serving our worldwide customers and I feel a sense of responsibility to our employees. Second, I live by a mantra, "When the going gets tough, I will quit tomorrow." For me, tomorrow has not come and so I continue to work diligently towards my goal. I realize that I may have to evolve and that my company may go through several life cycles before my goal is achieved. With patience, the right mix of employees, the willingness to let go and let grow -- inspiring creativity and innovation – and a little luck, success is just around the corner.

The only way you can win in the entrepreneur game is to participate! Remember, it's the fight that will keep you right. In the words of the late singer Michael Jackson, "Don't Stop 'til You Get Enough." I have heard many times that just when you are about to quit, success is staring at you around the corner. Finally, your plight is just that, your plight. If you decide to call it quits, do so because it is what you want to do and never look back. Otherwise, hold on to your dream and keep pushing forward.

Desired Actions or Goals I Will Take from Pointer 38

1. _____

_____

2. _____

_____

3. _____

_____

Be aware of the quiet ones. They are
the ones who actually think.
- Anonymous

How to Read a Room

Learning how to read a room during negotiations is a valuable skill to master. Many times, in our effort to get our points out, we fail to pay attention to how our information is being received by the participants. We are doing more speaking than observing the reactions of our audience. Are there one or two persons who are doing most of the interacting? Have you determined if they are the decision makers or the information seekers of the group? I have found that the quiet individuals in the room tend to hold more decision-making power. They are the ones I attempt to draw in, to ask questions of, and to seek their opinion or approval.

How can you tell who the decision makers are? They are generally the ones interested in the ROI, cost benefit analysis, lead time, cost, and payment terms. They rely on their team to flush out the feasibility of your proposal while they are focused on how to make it happen should their team agree on moving forward.

One tip I have learned is to do less talking and more listening. I give my pitch and then listen, further encouraging and promoting conversation from the group, keeping in mind to draw in everyone. At some point in the meeting, I always ask for approval. If I was seeking an order then I ask for the order, listen for any objections, respond to the objections, and then ask again for the order.

Desired Actions or Goals I Will Take from Pointer 39

1. _____

   _____

2. _____

   _____

3. _____

   _____

The common need is cash. Cash meets
payroll. Cash pays business loans.
— Stephen Moret

Making Payroll

O ne of the most difficult tasks of an entrepreneur is making payroll.
Ever wonder why some companies pay weekly, while others pay bi-
weekly or monthly? The payroll period is influenced early on by the
company's projected cash flow. If your business is one that brings in cash
daily, then a weekly or semi-weekly payroll may be appropriate. Companies
that rely on net thirty or greater payment terms may find bi-monthly or
monthly payroll to be more advantageous. In most states, companies with
part-time workers cannot pay monthly.

Keep in mind that payroll consists of the amount you need to pay each
employee, their deducted payroll taxes, and the company's portion. When
you pay your employees, you must also pay the associated payroll taxes to
the federal, state, or city, as required. It is important that you know that
cumulative number and plan for it. I recommend creating a separate payroll
bank account whereby you deposit receivables designated for payroll.

I have learned that the best way to avoid having payroll tax related
problems is to use a payroll service like Paychex, ADP, or Harpers Payroll
Services. There are a host of payroll services identified on the internet. The
benefits of using a payroll service are numerous. They issue the employee
checks; keep track of employee sick and vacation days; file federal, state and
city tax forms; make tax payments; and issue annual W-2 wage forms. It
takes a lot of discipline to bring the payroll function internally even if your
accounting software has a payroll module. With the consistent demands
for operating cash, it is much easier to create the habit of having sufficient

cash in the payroll account for periodic withdrawal from the payroll service versus commingling payroll with other operating expenses.

Making payroll is so important that I want to share some banking tips with you, as well. First, understand when your bank deposits are really available. Most banks are open Monday thru Friday with some having offices open on Saturday for shorter periods. At first glance, you may think you have five full business days to do business transactions. You only have four days where you have full banking services. With a one-day turnaround on bank deposits, checks deposited Monday thru Friday clear the next business day. If your bank is open on Saturday, you may get an extra day; however, checks deposited on Saturday, Sunday, or Monday will not have the deposited funds available until Tuesday. Be aware and learn how to use this to your benefit.

Secondly, some banks place holds on check deposits. There are numerous reasons for this occurrence but when it happens on a check you are depending on to make payroll, this can be devastating. This is when a positive relationship with your bank is important. You may be able to call your bank the day after depositing the check and ask for the funds to be released. In many cases, if the check is from a past customer or you have never had a deposited check returned, the bank will honor your request.

Desired Actions or Goals I Will Take from Pointer 40

1. _____

   _____

2. _____

   _____

3. _____

   _____

Faith doesn't make things easy, it makes them possible.
— Luke 1:37

Importance of Patents:
Trademarks and Copyrights

I f your business is based on a new product or invention that solves a problem, you may want to consider getting a patent, especially if it is a disruptive technology. If awarded, a patent can provide your company a barrier to entry for competition, potentially higher profit margins, protection from copying or theft, entrance into new market arenas, and litigation advantages. There are numerous articles on the internet on how to seek a patent. I recommend the following steps:

1. Maintain a careful record of your invention in a bound, numbered notebook. Date each entry and record all thought, research, and ideas relevant to your idea.

2. Check with a patent attorney to determine if your invention qualifies for patent protection.

3. Patent attorneys can be expensive, although experienced ones are worthy of their compensation, so a market potential of your invention should be performed. A preliminary financial upside determination will provide you with the financial information needed to make informed decisions on moving forward with your patent.

4. Write a description of your invention and send to at least three (3) reliable persons using USPS certified mail. Contact these persons

in advance to let them know you are sending a certified letter and <u>not</u> to open it, but to save for future reference.

5. Perform a detailed patent search to see if your invention is free of pre-existing patents.

6. Obtain a patent application, complete, and file with the United States Patent and Trademark Office (USPTO).

There are stringent rules about informing or selling your product prior to filing or receiving a patent. Should you file for patent pending? Talk with your legal advisor(s). Patents are assets; they provide value to your company. The flip side is that they take time to receive, are costly when using a patent attorney, and you are not protected from competitors copying your product if you elect to market it while your patent application is pending. I encourage you to use your advisory team when determining how and if you will patent your product(s).

When it comes to branding your product, i.e., naming it, it is important to understand trademarking and the difference between ™ and ® symbols. The former is non-registered and can be used to inform that this is a trademark of your company. The latter is robust because it is a registered trademark with the USPTO. There are federal laws regarding the use of registered trademarks and defense against infringement. There is no legal significance to using TM, however, it does notify the public of your claim of branding rights in a particular mark and can discourage your competitors from using the same mark for their similar products. Talk with legal counsel on the best ways to trademark your company and brand names.

Entrepreneurs who will be offering software-related solutions or products may consider copyrighting their software. Copyrights are processed by the Library of Congress U.S. Copyright Office in Washington, DC. At first glance, copyrighting software may seem advantageous, however, copyrighting software is tedious and there is no fool proof way to prevent piracy. My recommendation is that you focus more on getting revenue through sales of your software product(s) by licensing, private branding, and upgrades.

Over the years our focus was on branding our company through the sales of high-quality products and software. Our products have evolved over the thirty-plus years and, whereas we have experienced competitors who have attempted to duplicate our systems and software, we have managed to stay ahead of the competition because of our thorough understanding of our customer's needs. Our competitors sell equipment while we sell process solutions. There is a distinct difference in mentality and how our products and software are configured. My attitude has been that when competitors try to duplicate what you do, be flattered, and make sure that they are trying to catch up to you. Not the other way around. You can learn from your competition, but always position your company to be the leader in what you offer.

Desired Actions or Goals I Will Take from Pointer 41

1. _____

_____

2. _____

_____

3. _____

_____

Prepare the umbrella before it rains.
– Malay Proverb

Create and Maintain an Emergency Fund

Financial discipline is paramount to running a successful business. Yes, the sales team is important because there is no business without sales, however, managing your cash with all the business demands that require use of your cash is critical. Whether it is your incoming receivables or lines of credit, it is recommended that you set aside a small percentage – 5 to 10 percent -- in a separate business account that is your emergency fund. These monies are not available for normal business transactions; however, should you need access to these funds in an emergency or to take advantage of an unexpected opportunity, you treat them like a loan, not an installment loan, but one where a set interest is applied, and the monies are returned in a lump sum payment or whatever your cash flow will permit. Emergencies will occur from time-to-time and having an emergency fund allows you to financially deal with these issues in a timely manner with minimal impact on your daily operation. Talk with your accountant on how to establish an emergency fund for your business.

Desired Actions or Goals I Will Take from Pointer 42

1. _____

   _____

2. _____

   _____

3. _____

   _____

*Think left and think right and think low and think
high. Oh, the thinks you can think up if only you try.*
— Dr. Seuss

Guerilla Financing Techniques

Finding capital to support your business entity is a never-ending task for entrepreneurs. Traditional bank loans require collateral and are based on your Dun & Bradstreet business credit report. This also applies to banks offering SBA loans. I have found that the best time to secure a business loan or line of credit is when you don't need it. This may sound like an oxymoron but in truth when the business is doing well you are more apt to qualify for a traditional loan.

Credit cards are the easiest form of capital to acquire for your business. Obtaining credit cards is based on your personal credit score. As you use your credit card and payoff the balance most credit card companies will continually raise your credit limit. This form of financing requires strict discipline in paying off the balance monthly to avoid paying high credit card interest. I have found that the best credit card for business use is the American Express card. There is no preset limit, and you are required to pay of the balance monthly. The one drawback is that not all vendors or suppliers take AMEX cards. Check with your business bank and see what credit cards and credit limits they will afford your business.

Personal loans from friends or family are also an alternative. When borrowing money from these sources I recommend that you create a promissory agreement which clearly defines the amount borrowed, the interest that will be paid and the terms for repayment. My rule of thumb is that the interest offered on a personal loan should be at least three times the interest rate of your current bank's high yield CD rate. For example, if your bank is offering 1.5 percent on a high yield CD, then you should offer a fixed rate 4.5 percent on the monies you are borrowing. In doing so, you have now converted this personal loan into a business loan for both you and the lender. You no longer feel antsy about asking for a personal loan because it is a win-win for both parties. You get the loan you need to finance your business and they receive an interest on their monies greater than they can get at their bank.

Merchant cash advances, business cash advances, merchant loans, or whatever other name is used to offer a no collateral short term business loan are expensive. For example, one time I borrowed $15,000 and ended up paying $22,000 over a one-year period. These types of loans require you to complete an application and forward six months of your bank statements for review. They will generally fund a percentage of your average monthly deposits. Payment is daily. You agree to allow them to withdraw a set amount from your business bank account daily, Monday--Friday, less holidays and weekends until the loan is repaid. Once you inquire or acquire one of these loans you will be placed on a list and will be bombarded with calls from competing merchants. If you choose one of these loans, only borrow what you need and can afford to pay back.

Your customers and vendors are excellent sources of guerilla financing. When setting payment terms for an order from your customer, ask for scheduled payments. You may request terms such as 50 percent deposit, 15 percent after some critical event, 20 percent prior to shipment and the balance net thirty days. The point is to look at the financial requirements needed to fulfill an order and set your payment terms such that they will meet your obligations. Accepting an order at net thirty terms when you know you need cash to fulfill the order is not prudent. When purchasing materials from your vendor to satisfy an order, negotiate the payment terms with a clear understanding of how your client will be paying for the order. Communicate with your vendors and follow through on your payment agreements.

Desired Actions or Goals I Will Take from Pointer 43

1. _____

   _____

2. _____

   _____

3. _____

   _____

Raise the ceiling! Customers tend to gravitate
towards the middle of your price range.
– Scott Sorrell

The Pricing Model

One of the decisions entrepreneurs must make early on is how to price the products and services that they will be offering. Before pricing can be determined, a decision must be made on where on the Price / Quality curve you want your products and services to be viewed. In our case, we wanted to compete in the high price – high quality quadrant. This means that we would be asking a price higher than the competitive average and providing high quality products.

	Low	High
Quality	Low	High

Price

Next, competitive pricing analysis needs to be performed to get a feel on the price customers are willing to pay. A features, function, and benefits study on the competitor's products is required to compare your product offering with the competitor's. A value proposition for your product or service needs to be established. Can you quantify any potential savings the customer may realize in using your product or service? Savings can be in cycle time reduction, higher yields, labor savings, and increased market share, entrance into a new market segment, or faster time to market. Knowing your value proposition should support the prices you decide to charge.

There are several methods that can be used to derive at a selling price. One method is the cost-plus margin method. Here you determine your cost to produce the product and then add the desired profit margin. Web based businesses may give away the product or service to attract advertising dollars. Market pricing is when you charge what the market will bear regardless of your actual cost while ensuring your costs are covered. Other techniques include tiered or volume pricing and the printer and ink model – where the printer is sold at or below cost but there is a pricy consumable in the ink cartridge.

Pricing should not be static. It should be readjusted as you review the profitability of your business. Mr. Scott Sorrell, CEO of Sales Adrenaline, is known as Mr. Charge Higher Prices. I recommend you look him up on the internet to learn how your business can increase revenues through strategic charge higher pricing techniques.

Desired Actions or Goals I Will Take from Pointer 44

1. _____

   _____

2. _____

   _____

3. _____

   _____

Never tell people how to do things. Tell them what to
do and they will surprise you with their ingenuity.
— George Patton

Remember, You Already Have a Monkey

As an entrepreneur, you already have the responsibility to manage and grow your business. In other words, your business is your monkey. Knowing that you already have a monkey, and a large one at that, means you don't have to accept the monkeys brought to you by others. Monkeys are responsibilities that masquerade as problems. How can you spot a monkey? Simply watch what problems your employees bring to you and try to leave on or in your office. I encourage you to adopt a philosophy that is known throughout your organization that although you have an open-door policy and are open to discussing problems, it is clear that whatever monkeys are brought into your office leave with their owner.

Adopting this philosophy can minimize an entrepreneur's natural tendency to get involved with all aspects of their business. Specifically, it can cut down on micromanaging. It is a great tool to use to empower your employees. They can come and discuss a problem or situation knowing that at the conclusion of the meeting if the problem truly resides with them (it is understood that some problems presented may belong to another owner), they will leave with that problem. It is their monkey.

There was a supervisor at Hughes Aircraft Company, where I worked earlier in my career, who had a wooden monkey hanging from the hinges of his office door. One day I asked him why he had that monkey hanging and was told, "Oh, that's Joe. He is there to remind me and to let all who enter know that I already have a monkey." That statement had such an impact on me that when I left Hughes to start my own company, I asked if I could have Joe. He was given to me and I gave Joe a new home hanging from a picture frame behind my desk in my office.

Desired Actions or Goals I Will Take from Pointer 45

1. _____

    _____

2. _____

    _____

3. _____

    _____

Build a network of people who inspire, challenge,
and motivate you to make bold, fearless moves.
– Jo Miller

Networking: *The Benefits of Informal Hobnobbing*

There will be many times when you as the entrepreneur will feel alone. It is important for you to keep in mind that this is an illusion, not a fact. It is an indication that some aspect or problem that you are dealing with is being dealt with internally instead of outwardly. You may feel that presently you cannot take the situation to your advisory board for whatever reason, but you need to talk to someone. This is when having an informal group of advisors, mentors, or friends can be helpful. The group may meet from time-to-time for coffee or a sporting event like golf. During this time, you can bring up what is on your mind and gain the perspective of individuals who have no biases regarding your business but are open to talk freely about the topic you present. With the information received from this group, you may develop an action plan for yourself or decide to discuss the problem with your advisory board now that you have different points of view.

I have opened up to the owners of several of my vendor businesses. We talk about business problems ranging from cash flow to employee retention. I can garner a prospective from other business owners, many of whom have experienced similar situations that I am going through. We talk about our families, allotting time for vacations, pros and cons of different local banks, financing techniques, lease agreements and tenant improvements (TIs), and, of course, sports. I find each of them to be an invaluable source of information and support.

Desired Actions or Goals I Will Take from Pointer 46

1. _____

_____

2. _____

_____

3. _____

_____

Leadership is not a title. It is a behavior. Live it.
– Robin Sharma

When the Class is Failing, Look at the Teacher

You ever look at your organization or department within the enterprise and have trepidations about what you see? Are the employees in a department not following company policies the way you have defined them to your management? Do you get a sense that your team is not giving 100 percent or that customer service is not at the level you envision? We all have heard the phrase that entrepreneurs treat their company as their baby. Well, even babies evolve from infancy to toddler to teen to adulthood, and so do organizations and departments within organizations evolve. The frustrations occur when some of your departments or individuals are not evolving at the pace you desire or require to satisfy your customers.

When dysfunction, discord, work apathy or stagnation occurs the reason may not be the employees hired but the leaders responsible for those employees. Is your management team on the same page? Are they acting in an ego driven manner versus a results-oriented manner? Are the goals for each department clearly defined and the desired results clearly articulated? Are there metrics in place to clearly show the results from each department? You may find that you have a person in a management position that is not capable of getting the desired results and needs to be either trained or replaced. A closer look may reveal that you, the entrepreneur, are the problem. Expectations may not be clearly expressed or are overzealous. As entrepreneurs we tend to expect that our employees will be as passionate about the business as we are. When we don't see the passion, we may mistakenly equate it with a lack of effort resulting in our frustration. I have taught myself to take a step back and review the department. If the class is failing – several members of the department are not performing as expected – then I look at the teacher, the manager, or supervisor. If a group of the managers are not performing up to expectations, then I look at myself. What could I be doing or conveying differently that will lead the organization to achieve the desired results?

Desired Actions or Goals I Will Take from Pointer 47

1. _____

   _____

2. _____

   _____

3. _____

   _____

To some extent, being an entrepreneur is a lonely journey.
— Peter Drucker

Feeling the Pressure:
Not Seeing People Like You Out There

For those entrepreneurs who I am simply going to say are different (minorities, such as African Americans, Latinx, LBGTQI, Native American, etc.), there is a pressure that may be placed on you that brings challenges, attitudes, and uncomfortable situations. Dealing with people's biases, prejudices, cultural differences, resentments, and ignorance can be overwhelming at times. *What I say to you is to win despite these hurdles.* Don't let anyone or a group's behavior stop you from going after your dream. Integrity, competence, honesty, and humility will win every time.

I remember touring multiple facilities from a major lumber company around the US and at one location I was called "boy." I was startled when it first registered, but I was glad that I did not react to the salutation because it wasn't long that I heard another person, who did not look like me – in fact, he was a Caucasian – called the same name. At this facility, all the guys were referred to as "boy."

Going to trade shows over the years it was rare, if ever, that I saw any high-tech companies that were owned by someone who looked like me. For a long time, even the patrons of tech trade shows were less diverse. Today this is slowly changing. There are more high-tech companies with diverse owners and larger diverse attendees.

Be courageous. You don't have to take on the trailblazer mentality unless you want to. What is most important is that you be you. Stay focused on your goal, connect with those like you, embrace all who you meet, and enjoy your journey.

Desired Actions or Goals I Will Take from Pointer 48

1. _____

   _____

2. _____

   _____

3. _____

   _____

Corporate culture is the only sustainable competitive advantage
that is completely within the control of the entrepreneur.
— David Cummings

Importance of Creating Enterprise Maxims

Getting your organization to operate on the same page, regardless of situations or challenges, can be achieved through the use or implementation of corporate maxims. What is a maxim? A maxim is a belief, a fundamental principle, or a standard of conduct, that when thought of can help drive a decision or action.

From the very beginning of our company's evolution we have had several maxims that we live by. Below are ten key maxims that we rely on:

➢ "No one can out-think us when it comes to solving product identification marking problems." - This may sound cocky, but our belief is that if we as a team put our heads together, research what is available and visualize a solution, then we can solve virtually any product marking challenge presented to our team.

➢ "We are like Maytag. Our systems are built to last."

➢ "Simple is a compliment,"
– It takes hard work and attention to detail to make a system that customers say looks simple.

➢ "You don't need to go to a trade show to find customers. You should know who can use our products and services."
– Salespeople should know the type of companies and the positions held within those companies who would be interested in learning about our products and services. Trade shows are helpful but should not be relied upon to generate sales.

- ➤ "Everyone on our team is a professional. Act like one even when no one is looking"
- ➤ "Man Out"

  – As a manufacturer of product marking systems, we ship, install, and perform on-site start up and training worldwide. When one of our technicians is out performing system start-up, training or servicing they are considered out of the facility. We, the company as a team, have the responsibility to bring them home quickly. This means should they call or need assistance, that they have top company resource priority.

- ➤ "Existing customers take precedence over new or prospective customers."

  – Juggling limited resources can be a challenge and we never want our existing customers to feel that new or prospective customers are more important to us. Our employees are trained to give existing customers top priority.

- ➤ "Customers whose production is down take precedence,"

  – We understand that the marking process is taken for granted in most companies. Furthermore, that marking generally takes place at the last stage of production just prior to packaging and shipping. This means companies are banking on the fact that their products will be marked and shipped in a relative short time span. When our equipment goes down, we have impacted our customer's ability to make shipments. We take this seriously and thus our employees are trained to ask if production is down when we receive calls for servicing. This helps us to prioritize our limited resources.

- ➤ "When problems occur in the field, always portray confidence that the problem will be fixed."

  – Many times, when a technician is out in the field, unexpected problems occur. Problems where it is apparent that the technician does not have an immediate solution. We train our technicians to stay calm, to use all their resources – including "Man Out" – but most important, to stay confident that the problem will be resolved. Confidence under pressure is a key trait that wins customer loyalty.

- ➤ "Never come to a staff meeting without your notebook."
- ➤ – Staff meetings are where information is shared, and tasks are delineated to individuals. We don't expect our employees to remember everything, but we do expect them to record information specific for them.

Desired Actions or Goals I Will Take from Pointer 49

1. _____

   _____

2. _____

   _____

3. _____

   _____

Most of all, I discovered that in order to succeed with a product you must truly get to know your customers and build something for them.
– Marc Benioff

When to Be Like Your Customer

There are times when it is advantageous to think, dress, and act like the customer you are serving. If you are selling nationally to manufacturing firms, like I have over the years, then you need to be aware of the intercultural differences between the locations within the same company. Don't assume all Boeing, Northrop Grumman, or Georgia Pacific facilities are the same from location to location. The corporate policies may be identical; however, employees bring their regional or demographic cultures with them to work resulting in changes in communication and interaction styles. Some homework may be required when attempting to promote sales of your products and services to companies located in different demographics. Some require you to dress like them to fit in. Blue collar may mean blue jeans and if you are sporting professional suited attire you may feel like an outcast.

I have found it beneficial to feel the people I am prospecting or servicing, showing empathy for their situation. I put myself in their shoes to fully understand the challenges they are facing. For example, a quality manager is having trouble getting a product past their source inspector. I not only want to know what problems the source inspector is exposing, but also what impact is this having with the QA's management and production team. What resources – people, time, capital – are being expended to satisfy the situation? My goal is to understand what my prospect is going through so that I can offer a more complete solution, if available. This type of approach allows my customer to feel supported and understood, and generally results in a long-term business relationship.

Desired Actions or Goals I Will Take from Pointer 50

1. _____

   _____

2. _____

   _____

3. _____

   _____

No matter how great the talent or efforts, some things just take time. You can't produce a baby in one month by getting nine women pregnant.
-Warren Buffett

So, Just How Long Does It Take to Create an Effective Website?

For many businesses, their website is their most prominent tool to achieve sales, but the attention placed on creating and updating the website is minimal. There seems to be a misalignment between marketing / sales and the IT department responsible for the website. It takes nine months to bring a baby into this world, but far longer to create an effective website. With the tools available launching a website can be quick. What takes time is the preparation! It should start with your management team asking the question, "What is the purpose of our website"? How do we get the traffic to our site to take our desired action? If you are updating or creating a brand-new website, how do you properly do a redirect using a 301 redirect or a temporary 302 redirect? So many websites are information websites that are cumbersome to either navigate or to take action to purchase the products or services shown. Many websites forget that now that they have captured the eyeballs of the viewers to include a clear call to action.

My research shows that it can "take between 90-180 days, depending on the competitiveness of the industry and popularity of your keywords" to jump to the front of Google's results. And that is if the website was created by a knowledgeable team using an experienced SEO. Upping your Google rankings requires consistent work and retailoring of the website and can take upwards of one year or more to see the desired results.

I strongly recommend that if you are planning on creating a new website or updating an existing one, that you start by contracting with a search engine optimization (SEO) firm. They will guide you through going from where you are now to launching that effective website complete with results metrics. They can help with keywords, including reverse keyword searches; page optimization; the proper inclusion of social media, like Twitter, Instagram, and Facebook. With the information obtained, you now can interview potential web designers and talk specifically on how your website needs to be constructed based on your business objectives.

There are a lot of companies that can make websites for your business. You must decide who will create the website, where will it be hosted, do you want an email server from your website host, and in which language your site will be written in (HTML, Word Press, Java, JavaScript, Python, etc.) Do you want the capability to make changes to your site or will you require assistance each time a change or update is desired? Regardless of what tools are used to create the site, do not lose sight that the goal of the website is to make sure that when a potential prospect is looking for the products and services you offer, that they find you quickly and take action to secure or get information on the products and services they are viewing. Finally, you have done the work to capture the eyeballs of prospective clients and it is equally important to keep them at your site. Partner links are excellent, however, make sure that your viewers are redirected back to your website for action.

Desired Actions or Goals I Will Take from Pointer 51

1. _____

   _____

2. _____

   _____

3. _____

   _____

If you know how to beg, we may have a position
for you in Accounts Receivable.
- Glasbergen

Accounts Receivable:
Your Hidden Source of Cash

Entrepreneurs are so focused on growing their businesses that they fail to keep their eye on the accounts receivable aging and balances. The organization has secured the sale, delivered the product or service, but has not followed up on getting paid. There are many reasons why invoices are not paid in a timely manner. Some of them include: invoice has never been received; the purchase order number on the invoice does not match; the invoice has not been entered into your customer's system; a matching packing slip has not been received; there is a discrepancy on the invoice; and it is with management for approval. Regardless of the reason, YOU have not been paid.

I have found that a good, effective collections person pays for themselves. They create relationships with the accounts payable person from your slow paying accounts and in many cases can move your company higher on their payment priority. Today, email is the primary method of business-to-business communication, however, a telephone call to the accounts payable person can be more effective.

ACH is the best form of payment. Funds are transferred to your corporate bank account and you are notified via email when the payment will be made. Credit card payments can be costly, but you can receive your funds faster. Many companies prefer to pay with credit cards to take advantage of credit card offerings and to avoid using their current cash. When collecting older invoices, provide your UPS or FedEx number to your customer so you can receive payment quicker. This also eliminates the infamous "check is in the mail" or lost check scenarios.

Desired Actions or Goals I Will Take from Pointer 52

1. _____

   _____

2. _____

   _____

3. _____

   _____

Printed in the United States
By Bookmasters